Original title:
Harmony's Journey

Copyright © 2025 Swan Charm
All rights reserved.

Author: Liisi Lendorav
ISBN HARDBACK: 978-1-80560-096-1
ISBN PAPERBACK: 978-1-80560-561-4

Whirling Leaves of Mutual Understanding

In autumn's dance, leaves twirl and spin,
Golden whispers share the tales within.
Beneath the trees, hearts begin to meld,
In silence, truths of friendship are upheld.

Each gust of wind, a message softly sent,
Kindred spirits rise, while shadows blend.
Nature's chorus hums, a sweet refrain,
In whirling leaves, we find joy and pain.

The Lullaby of Joined Journeys

In twilight's glow, we share a sweet sigh,
With voices low, we let our dreams fly.
A lullaby woven from hearts that care,
Together we travel, stripped of despair.

On winding paths, we find solace and grace,
As stars awaken, lighting our place.
Joined in our journeys, we craft our song,
In the hush of night, where we all belong.

Where Soft Winds Meet

In fields where whispers play,
The gentle winds do sway.
Each blade does softly bend,
Where quiet moments blend.

The sun dips low in grace,
With shadows we embrace.
A dance of light and shade,
In nature's calm parade.

The flowers nod in peace,
As busy thoughts release.
In harmony they sway,
Where soft winds find their way.

Beneath the vast blue dome,
We find our hearts a home.
In unity, we greet,
The magic at our feet.

The Lotus of Intertwined Paths

Amidst the misty morn,
Two souls together born.
In waters deep and clear,
Their destinies draw near.

The lotus blooms so pure,
A bond that's strong and sure.
With roots beneath the waves,
Their hearts the current saves.

Through trials they will wade,
In love's sweet serenade.
Two paths merge into one,
As life's great race is run.

In whispers, secrets shared,
With every glance, they cared.
The beauty of their quest,
In union, they find rest.

Cadence of the Open Heart

In evening's gentle glow,
The heart begins to know.
A rhythm soft and true,
In every beat anew.

With open arms we stand,
To greet love's warm command.
A dance of pure delight,
As stars adorn the night.

Each laugh and tear we share,
Creates a bond so rare.
The cadence of our song,
Together we belong.

Through every joy and pain,
In sunshine, in the rain.
A symphony we weave,
In love, we dare believe.

Dreamscapes of Interwoven Souls

In twilight's soft embrace,
Two spirits find their space.
In dreams, their whispers blend,
Where shadows gently mend.

They travel worlds unseen,
In realms of silver sheen.
With every step they take,
A magic they will make.

Through valleys deep and wide,
Together they will glide.
In each enchanted scene,
The bond between them gleans.

In laughter, in despair,
They weave a tale so rare.
Through dreamscapes they will soar,
Two souls forevermore.

The Gentle Tug of Interwoven Destinies

In the quiet of the night,
Two hearts pull gently near,
Threads of fate softly sewn,
Destinies intertwine here.

Whispers carried by the breeze,
Promises in the moonlight,
Every heartbeat, every sigh,
Brings the future into sight.

Paths once walked alone,
Now converge with tender grace,
Every shadow, every light,
Leads us to this sacred space.

Hands may tremble, eyes may shine,
In this dance, we find our way,
The gentle tug of time and space,
We are woven, come what may.

With every challenge we embrace,
Through storms, we boldly tread,
Hope a compass, love a guide,
In this journey, we are wed.

Unfolding Petals of Togetherness

In a garden rich with dreams,
Petals rise, unfurling slow,
Each moment a subtle wink,
Of love's radiant, soft glow.

Hands entwined, laughter shared,
Every glance a spark ignites,
Sunlight dances on our skin,
Life blooms in enchanting sights.

Through the seasons, we will grow,
Roots intertwined, strong and deep,
In the warmth of tender care,
Promises we'll forever keep.

Raindrops fall, we breathe anew,
Nurtured by the storms we've faced,
Unfolding petals, side by side,
In this beauty, we are graced.

Let the world fade into night,
Together, we will brightly shine,
In this garden of our hearts,
Love's fragrance will intertwine.

The Light After the Ascent

After mountains high we climb,
With weary hearts and tired feet,
A glow breaks forth on the horizon,
In that moment, life feels sweet.

Though the path was rough and steep,
Every struggle carved new grace,
The summit shines with golden rays,
Illuminating our embrace.

In the silence, peace descends,
Clouds part gently, skies unfold,
We stand together, breathless, still,
The light of dreams begins to hold.

Every tear and every smile,
A testament to what we've fought,
In the warmth of love's embrace,
All the battles fade to naught.

Together we have reached this place,
In the glow, we find our way,
The light that graced our journey,
Will lead us through each new day.

Uncharted Waters of Connection

Sailing forth on seas unknown,
With hearts as anchors cast,
Each wave whispers secrets deep,
As the winds of fate blow past.

Beneath the stars, we chart a course,
Through storms, and sunlit days,
In uncharted waters we drift,
Lost in love's mysterious ways.

Every glance a compass point,
Every smile a gentle sail,
Together through the fiercest tides,
In this bond, we will prevail.

When darkness cloaks the sky above,
And doubts begin to creep,
We'll navigate the unknown seas,
With promises we keep.

For in these waters wild and free,
Connection guides our way,
In the depths of love's embrace,
Every heartbeat leads the day.

Melodies of Coexistence

In sunlit fields where flowers bloom,
Voices blend, dispelling gloom.
Every note, a gentle sway,
Together we find our way.

Rivers whisper secrets low,
Winds of change begin to blow.
Hearts entwined, a radiant sound,
In harmony, we are found.

Beneath the stars, a shared delight,
Every dream, a beacon bright.
Hands reach out, community grows,
In every heartbeat, love flows.

Through storms and trials, we stand fast,
Creating futures, strong and vast.
With open arms, we celebrate,
Embracing all, we cultivate.

In unity, our spirits soar,
Together, always seeking more.
The melody of life's embrace,
A symphony of every race.

The Dance of Echoing Souls

In twilight's glow, we find our feet,
A gentle rhythm, soft and sweet.
With every step, a tale we weave,
In shared laughter, we believe.

The moonlight glimmers on the floor,
A whispered promise, nothing more.
Shadows play, weaving their art,
In every move, we weave our heart.

Around us, time begins to blur,
In silent tunes, our visions stir.
Echoes bounce, a tender sound,
In this space, we're homeward bound.

With open arms, we take the chance,
In every sway, we breathe and dance.
Together, lost in night's embrace,
We echo dreams, our sacred space.

In the stillness, passion glows,
With every beat, our spirit flows.
The dance of souls, forever true,
In unity, I find you.

Threads of Unity Woven

Across the world, a tapestry,
Of colors bright, in harmony.
Each thread a story, rich and smart,
We weave together, heart to heart.

In every stitch, a dream is spun,
Together, we shine like the sun.
With hands entwined, we labor on,
In every dawn, a brand-new song.

A fabric strong, it holds us tight,
In shadows deep, it brings us light.
With every knot, a bond we share,
A legacy of love and care.

Through trials faced and paths we roam,
In unity, we find our home.
With open hearts, we share our fears,
We stitch our hopes across the years.

In every pattern, life's design,
A wondrous blend of yours and mine.
Together woven, bold and bright,
We light the world with shared delight.

Whispers in the Breezy Canvas

Beneath the sky, the colors play,
In gentle whispers, night and day.
The breeze carries soft secrets near,
In every sigh, the world draws near.

From leaves that dance to oceans wide,
Voices merge and gently glide.
In fleeting moments, beauty speaks,
In harmony, our spirit peaks.

The canvas stretches, vast and clear,
Each stroke a memory, ever dear.
With every breath, the world unfolds,
In quietude, our truth beholds.

As twilight wraps the day's embrace,
We find our peace, our sacred space.
In whispers light, the heart takes wing,
With every sound, new life we bring.

In breezes soft, our dreams take flight,
Guided by stars, we chase the light.
Together we paint this life anew,
In whispers shared, we dream with you.

Pebbles on the Path of Understanding

Small stones lie underfoot,
Each one tells a tale,
Whispers of the journey,
Guiding us without fail.

The path may twist and blend,
With shadows, light, and shade,
Yet every stone a friend,
In the choices we have made.

Stepping stones of wisdom,
Crackled, worn, and gray,
They teach us with silence,
To find our own way.

Hearts like pebbles, resting,
In pools of untold dreams,
Reflecting life's great lessons,
Beneath the moonlit beams.

Each click, each gentle roll,
A sound to softly hear,
The path of understanding,
Is walked with those we hold dear.

The Bliss of Unexpected Companionship

In quiet moments, laughter blooms,
Like flowers breaking ground,
Two souls meet in serendipity,
In joy, they are unbound.

Paths crossed on a rainy day,
Umbrellas side by side,
With shared warmth and smiles to trade,
In each, a trusted guide.

Strangers once, now kindred hearts,
In stories intertwined,
Every glance a spark ignites,
In closeness redesigned.

Through seasons ebbing, flowing,
Together they will stand,
Finding bliss in moments sweet,
In life's uncharted land.

A bond that formed unexpectedly,
Like a sunbeam in the mist,
Reminds us of the treasure found,
In friendship's gentle twist.

Sails of Togetherness on the Wide Ocean

On waters deep and wide,
Two sails catch the breeze,
In harmony they glide,
As waves dance with ease.

The horizon, painted colors bright,
A canvas made for two,
With each gust, they take flight,
In adventures born anew.

Together through the stormy seas,
In trust, they find their way,
Linked by hope and memories,
They face each dawning day.

With laughter shared and quiet times,
Their hearts remain as one,
Underneath the endless skies,
Their journey's just begun.

Sails of togetherness unfurled,
Carried by dreams untold,
In the vastness of the world,
Their love is purest gold.

The Murmurs of Serene Waters

In stillness, waters whisper low,
A song of peace and calm,
Ripples weave a gentle flow,
Nature's soothing balm.

Beneath the trees, in soft embrace,
The lake reflects the sky,
A tranquil haven, a sacred space,
Where time seems to pass by.

Murmurs of the ancient tales,
Speak softly to the shore,
Tales of dreams that never fail,
To linger evermore.

Crickets play a quiet tune,
As stars begin to gleam,
The night wraps round like a cocoon,
Inviting us to dream.

In the grasp of serene waters,
Life's worries drift away,
Here, love and peace can flourish,
At the close of every day.

Lyricism of Falling Leaves

Whispers from the trees, they sway,
In hues of amber, gold, they play.
Each leaf a story, drifting down,
A symphony of autumn's crown.

Beneath the sky, a canvas vast,
Time sings softly, shadows cast.
Their journey dances on the breeze,
In this quiet, nature's ease.

Rustling gently, secrets shared,
In the quiet, hearts are bared.
Embracing change in fleeting flight,
The leaves beckon, a warm goodnight.

Crimson, russet, shades of fire,
A fleeting spark of kind desire.
They remind us to let go, too,
In every ending, life anew.

As branches stand, the earth below,
Holds memories of summers' glow.
With every fall, we learn to rise,
In nature's arms, our spirits fly.

The Soul's Gentle Interlude

In the hush where shadows dwell,
A soft tale begins to swell.
Moments linger, sweet and still,
The soul awakens to its will.

Gentle whispers echo low,
In the heart where dreams do flow.
Silvery threads of thought unwind,
In this space, peace we find.

Fleeting thoughts like clouds drift by,
Soft reflections in the sky.
Each sigh a lesson, every pause,
A gentle nudge, a quiet cause.

As twilight dances, dusk descends,
The soul, unravels, it transcends.
Finding rhythms, tender and kind,
In every silence, truth aligned.

Here in stillness, we ignite,
A flicker of the inner light.
The soul's interlude, pure delight,
Guiding us through the velvet night.

Serene Routes to Wholeness

Winding paths beneath the trees,
Softly rustling in the breeze.
Each step brings a tranquil grace,
Nature's rhythm, a warm embrace.

The sun peeks through the canopy,
Lighting the way, setting free.
Every journey, a chance to grow,
In stillness, inner truths flow.

With every breath, we find our peace,
Fragments of self, slowly release.
In nature's arms, we're whole again,
Healing whispers, a gentle refrain.

The brook's babble sings of dreams,
In its waters, our hopes gleam.
Among the flowers, spirits mend,
On these routes, we find our friends.

As dusk blankets the earth in gold,
Our stories shared, a bond retold.
In serene moments, hearts entwine,
Paths of wholeness, so divine.

The Song of Shared Futures

In the dawn, our voices rise,
Together painting endless skies.
Dreams entwined, a vision bright,
A tapestry of shared delight.

Each note we sing, a bond we weave,
In the rhythm of those who believe.
Hands united, strong and free,
Building tomorrows, you and me.

As seasons change, we stand as one,
Facing storms, embracing the sun.
With every challenge, our hearts soar,
In every triumph, we seek more.

The melodies of hope resound,
In every heartbeat, love is found.
Together, we embrace the chance,
To dance in life's exquisite dance.

Through trials and joys, we navigate,
The song of futures we create.
In harmony, we carve our way,
A brighter dawn awaits each day.

Dance of the Painted Horizons

In twilight's glow, colors blend,
Whispers of evening softly send,
A dance of hues, rich and bright,
Crafting the canvas of night.

With every stroke, the shadows twine,
Beneath the brush, destinies align,
A serenade of light takes flight,
In the embrace of fading light.

Golden suns and sapphire skies,
Swirling dreams where silence lies,
Eternity within a glance,
A painted world begins to dance.

Catch the spark in the cool night air,
Feel the rhythm, lose your care,
Each star a note in the cosmic song,
In harmony, we all belong.

So sway beneath the painted dome,
In this vast world, find your home,
Let the colors guide your feet,
In the rhythm, life's heartbeat.

Blessings Under the Shared Sun

In the morning light, hearts arise,
With golden rays that touch the skies,
Together, we bloom and grow,
Blessed by the warmth's gentle flow.

Hands entwined in shared embrace,
Each smile reflects a sacred space,
The laughter dances on the breeze,
In unity, we find our peace.

Through trials and joys that entwine,
Strengthened roots in the divine,
Under the shared sun's bright call,
We rise together, never fall.

As shadows linger, hope ignites,
In the stillness, love unites,
Together, we break every chain,
Finding beauty in the pain.

With every sunset's gentle hue,
We count the blessings, old and new,
Guided by the stars above,
Together forever, in light and love.

The Vibration of Mutual Dreams

In silent whispers, dreams collide,
Hearts in tune, side by side,
Echoes of hope in every breath,
Binding souls, defying death.

A symphony of thoughts aligned,
In visions bright, the stars have shined,
Weaving tapestries, hearts entwined,
In the canvas of the mind.

With every heartbeat, dreams expand,
In this rhythm, we make our stand,
The pulse of life, it gently sways,
To the melody that plays.

Reach for the light that we create,
In every chance, we celebrate,
With laughter's glow and tears' release,
Building bridges, finding peace.

Together in this world so wide,
Through every storm, our dreams abide,
In vibrations strong, we rise as one,
Forever bound until we're done.

The Convergence of Distant Stars

In the velvet night, they gather near,
From far-off worlds, bright and clear,
A symphony of light unfolds,
In stories whispered, truth is told.

Across the expanse, journeys blend,
Fates intertwined, the cosmos bends,
With each twinkle, a promise bright,
Guiding lost souls in the night.

In shadows cast, the dreams unite,
Fires igniting, hearts take flight,
Destiny calls from the heavens above,
Drawing us close with threads of love.

Infinite paths, yet we find a way,
To navigate the light of day,
In every glance, a spark ignites,
Creating magic on starry nights.

So watch the skies, let your spirit soar,
In every twinkle, find what's in store,
In convergence, our futures merge,
With distant stars, let hope surge.

The Language of Quiet Moments

In the hush before the dawn,
Whispers of the heart are drawn.
Stars fade into gentle light,
Softly bidding dreams goodnight.

In stillness, silence speaks so clear,
Each breath confides what we hold dear.
Time slows down, a soothing balm,
Embracing peace, a tender calm.

Thoughts entwined in sweet repose,
Within, a garden gently grows.
Moments linger, soft and bright,
Cradled in the arms of night.

A single tear, a laugh, a sigh,
Echoes of the by-and-bye.
In quietude, the soul can dance,
Finding joy in every chance.

Beneath the weight of gentle stars,
We ponder dreams and destiny's scars.
In silence, life unfolds its page,
A vibrant story, wisdom's sage.

Navigating the Sea of Kindred Spirits

Waves of laughter kiss the shore,
Hearts aligned forevermore.
In the depths of honest eyes,
Friendship sails, the spirit flies.

Navigating through the tide,
With each heartbeat, love's our guide.
Stars are shining in the night,
Anchored souls, a shared delight.

In the currents, we collide,
Finding treasures deep inside.
Voices mingle, fears take flight,
Together, we embrace the light.

Islands formed by tender hands,
Creating trust where friendship stands.
On this voyage, paths entwine,
A dance of fate, by design.

Across horizons, sails unfurl,
Unified, we spin and twirl.
In this sea of hearts, we find,
The strength that binds us, intertwined.

Bridges of Compassion

Two hearts reaching, hands extended,
In the void where love is blended.
Bridges built on empathy,
Together we can stand and see.

Through storms of life, we're never lost,
The warmth of care, the human cost.
Each act of kindness, a gentle thread,
Weaving hope where hearts can tread.

In every tear and every smile,
Our burdens shared, we walk a mile.
With open arms, we greet the day,
In bridges made, we find our way.

Compassion flows, a river wide,
Uniting souls on either side.
In every heart, a story shared,
A promise held that none is spared.

Together we can light the night,
Transforming shadows into light.
With every step, we pave the path,
In bridges built, we find our math.

A Tapestry of Light

Threads of gold in twilight spun,
Weaving stories, one by one.
Colors dance in vibrant hues,
A canvas rich with dreams infused.

Each stitch a moment, finely placed,
In every heart, the fabric traced.
A tapestry of joy and pain,
Bright threads entwined, love's sweet gain.

Gentle hands with care create,
In patterns woven, never late.
Whispers of a life well-lived,
In every knot, the heart is sieve.

Under the glow of evening's grace,
We celebrate the truth we face.
In every fiber, hope takes flight,
A wondrous blend, our shared light.

Together, we will build and mend,
A tapestry that knows no end.
With every laugh and every tear,
We craft the fabric we hold dear.

Journey Through the Garden of Voices

In a garden where whispers dwell,
Colors bloom, their stories tell.
Every petal, a tale to share,
Echoes linger in the air.

Winds of change gently blow,
Secrets in the seeds do grow.
Each step taken, a note in time,
Nature's chorus, pure and prime.

Sunlight dapples through the leaves,
Carefully weaving, life achieves.
With each voice that comes alive,
Hope and dreams begin to thrive.

Fluttering wings dance around,
In this haven, joy is found.
Listen closely, hear the song,
In unity, we all belong.

The night will fall, the stars ignite,
Guiding us with their gentle light.
Together, hearts and voices rise,
In this garden, love never dies.

Embrace Beneath the Starlit Sky

Under a blanket of twinkling light,
Two souls meet in the soft twilight.
Hand in hand, they wander free,
In the realm of eternity.

Whispers dance on the evening air,
Promises woven without a care.
Every heartbeat sings a rhyme,
In this moment, lost in time.

As constellations begin to glow,
Dreams unfold, the love will grow.
Eyes reflect the cosmic play,
In stardust dreams, they choose to stay.

The moonlight casts a silver beam,
Lighting paths of hope and dream.
With every sigh, the night unfolds,
In secrets shared, their passion holds.

Together they trace the stars above,
In that silence, they find their love.
The universe, vast and wide,
Could never hold their hearts inside.

The Compass of Kindness

In a world filled with shades of gray,
A little kindness lights the way.
Gentle words, a caring touch,
Can change a heart that needs it much.

Through storms of doubt, and winds of fear,
Compassion breaks boundaries, draws near.
When burdens heavy weigh us down,
A smile can turn the tide around.

Like ripples drawn upon the sea,
Acts of kindness return, you see.
The compass points to what is right,
Illuminate the darkest night.

In every heart, a spark ignites,
When we share those tender sights.
Hand in hand, we'll journey on,
A world reborn, a brighter dawn.

So let your heart be open wide,
In every moment, let love guide.
Together, we can rise above,
With the compass of our love.

Lindy Hop of Life's Tapestry

In the dance of life, joy takes flight,
Every step brings pure delight.
We twirl and spin, hearts in sync,
A melody that makes us think.

Threads of laughter intertwine,
Giving color to the divine.
With every beat, our spirits soar,
In this rhythm, we ask for more.

The past and future blend as one,
In vibrant hues, our tales begun.
Together we craft each moment rare,
In the tapestry, love is laid bare.

With every dip, we find our place,
Ebbing, flowing, in life's embrace.
Hand in hand, through thick and thin,
In this Lindy Hop, our joys begin.

So let's waltz into the unknown,
In every step, we've brightly grown.
Together, we weave our dance so grand,
Life's tapestry, forever hand in hand.

Confluence of Heartbeats

In the quiet of the night, we meet,
Two souls intertwined, gentle and sweet.
With every glance, the world fades away,
A symphony plays, in love's soft sway.

Whispers exchanged, secrets unfold,
A tapestry woven, stories retold.
In the pulse of the moment, we find our way,
A dance of two hearts, come what may.

Beneath the stars, our dreams take flight,
In the embrace of hope, everything feels right.
Together we shine, like constellations bright,
In this confluence, we bask in the light.

Through storms we wander, hand in hand,
With faith as our compass, we make our stand.
In the rhythm of love, we learn, we grow,
Together as one, wherever we go.

Each heartbeat a promise, pure and true,
In this beautiful journey, just me and you.
With every moment, we carve our path,
In the confluence of heartbeats, we find our math.

Rhythms of Serendipity

In the dance of chance, we find our way,
Fates align, as night turns to day.
With laughter and light, our spirits collide,
In the rhythms of serendipity, we ride.

Unexpected smiles, and the spark of a glance,
Life's sweet surprises, a whimsical dance.
Together we twirl, in a joyous embrace,
Finding our bliss in this magical space.

With every heartbeat, the world sings anew,
Colors awaken, and skies turn blue.
In the embrace of the moment, we surrender,
In the rhythms of life, we grow ever fonder.

Paths intertwine, like threads in a loom,
Creating a tapestry, banishing gloom.
With serendipity guiding, we leap and we fly,
In this joyous adventure, together we try.

Through valleys of doubt, and mountains of fear,
Love whispers softly, always right here.
In the geometry of chance, we revel and glide,
In the rhythms of serendipity, side by side.

Bridge Over Murmuring Waters

A bridge built of dreams spans the flowing stream,
Where whispers of water weave a soft theme.
In the murmur of currents, our hopes intertwine,
Together we wander, your hand in mine.

Underneath our feet, the river does flow,
Carrying secrets only we know.
Each step that we take, with purpose and grace,
We find in this moment, our sacred space.

The sun paints the skies in colors divine,
As we traverse this bridge, our spirits align.
In the echo of laughter, we fade into night,
On this bridge over waters, our hearts feel the light.

With every soft ripple, a promise is made,
In the calm of the evening, our dreams are displayed.
On this bridge of connection, no fear left to mar,
For in love's gentle flow, we've traveled so far.

As the stars watch above, we continue to glide,
With the strength of our bond, we both feel the tide.
On this bridge of our making, we savor the view,
In the depth of connection, just me and you.

Tides of Shared Dreams

On shores of imagination, we gather our hopes,
Sailing on tides, through life's endless scopes.
With every wave crashing, a story unfolds,
In the richness of dreams, our future is told.

The moon casts its glow, lighting up the sea,
In the silence of night, just you and me.
With hearts wide open, we venture afar,
On this journey together, we're each other's star.

Waves whisper secrets, carried by the breeze,
In this dance of creation, we move with ease.
With laughter and courage, we conquer our fears,
On the tides of our dreams, we splash through the years.

With each rising sun, a new chance to soar,
In the sea of our visions, we're destined for more.
Together we'll sail, through storm and through calm,
In the tides of shared dreams, we've found our balm.

As the stars blanket night, we hold on so tight,
In the expanse of our dreams, everything feels right.
With faith as our guide and love as our theme,
We navigate the waters of our shared dream.

Unraveling Threads of Peace

In quiet corners, whispers grow,
Where hope entwines with seeds we sow.
Each thread a promise in the light,
Together weaving peace through night.

With every hand that reaches out,
We stitch a world beyond all doubt.
In gentle warmth, our dreams expand,
Creating bonds that softly stand.

The tapestry of hearts aligned,
With laughter shared, our souls combined.
In unity, we rise and mend,
For peace is found in every friend.

Through trials faced, we learn to trust,
In fragile threads, our hearts combust.
Each moment crafted, bright and clear,
A tapestry of love sincere.

So let us gather, spark the flame,
In every heart, we'll find our name.
Together weaving, step by step,
Unraveling threads, we do not forget.

The Garden of Shared Dreams

In a garden where hopes intertwine,
We sow our dreams, both yours and mine.
With every seed, a vision grows,
In gentle whispers, the heart knows.

Amongst the flowers, we find delight,
Each petal glows with shared insight.
Together tending, nurturing care,
A sanctuary beyond compare.

In sunlight's dance, we laugh and play,
Beneath the stars, we weave our way.
With roots entwined, our spirits rise,
In unity, we touch the skies.

The blooms of joy, the scents of peace,
In every moment, worries cease.
We harvest hope with every beam,
In this, our garden, we shall dream.

So wander here, where paths converge,
In the garden, our souls emerge.
With hands united, hearts entwined,
We'll cultivate the love we find.

Embers of Understanding

In the glow of twilight's grace,
Embarking on a profound embrace.
Each ember whispers tales of old,
In the fire's warmth, we are bold.

With every spark, the darkness fades,
Connecting hearts through gentle fades.
In stories shared, we find our way,
Illuminating each other's day.

Like rivers flowing, we must bend,
In shared understanding, we transcend.
Through dialogue, our fears dissolve,
In unity, our hearts evolve.

The flicker of truth lights the night,
Igniting warmth, dispelling fright.
Together, we will rise and stand,
With embers glowing, hand in hand.

So gather 'round, let voices blend,
In the conversation, we will mend.
With every word, respect we'll send,
As embers flicker, hearts extend.

Wings of Tranquility

With wings of calm, we start to soar,
Above the noise, to distant shore.
In peaceful silence, we shall glide,
On gentle breezes, side by side.

The melody of whispers calls,
As tranquility softly falls.
In every beat, our hearts align,
A symphony of hope divine.

Through fields of dreams, we float with grace,
In every moment, we find our place.
With open wings, we learn to trust,
In the journey, gold from dust.

As sunsets fade to twilight's hue,
In tranquil realms, our spirits renew.
With every heartbeat, love we share,
In harmony, we banish despair.

So spread your wings, embrace the night,
With calmest hearts, we'll find our light.
In tranquil skies, we'll rise and play,
With wings of peace, we'll find our way.

Woven Threads of Connection

In the quiet, hearts entwine,
Silent whispers, soft as wine.
Threads of time, both old and new,
Stitched together, me and you.

Each encounter, a gentle thread,
Crafting stories yet unsaid.
Fingers trace the patterns we weave,
In these bonds, we learn to believe.

Through the distance, love remains,
Filling spaces, breaking chains.
Woven tight, like fabric strands,
Together still, when time demands.

In laughter shared and sorrows shared,
The tapestry of life declared.
Woven threads, no end in sight,
In every heart, a spark of light.

So let us cherish, let us hold,
Each moment shared, a tale retold.
In woven threads, we find our place,
A web of love, a warm embrace.

Ripples in the Stillness

In quiet ponds, the world reflects,
Whispers soft, yet deeply affects.
Each ripple born from tender touch,
Echoing life, it means so much.

Moments linger, then drift away,
In stillness, thoughts of yesterday.
A gentle hand upon the face,
Ripples formed in this sacred space.

Time flows like water, smooth and clear,
Every glance, a bond held near.
In silence, secrets dare to flow,
Ripples dance, as feelings grow.

So listen close to the quiet hum,
In the stillness, we become.
Each wave a note in life's grand song,
Ripples guide us, where we belong.

In every heart, a stillness beats,
In every soul, a space that meets.
Together we make the softest sound,
Ripples echo, love unbound.

The Dance of Interwoven Lives

Step by step, we find our way,
In the dance, night turns to day.
Swirling ribbons, bright and bold,
Stories shared, and hands to hold.

Each encounter, a graceful turn,
In the flame, our spirits burn.
Twisting, twirling, lost in time,
An unbroken, silent rhyme.

Footfalls echo with every glance,
In harmony, we take our chance.
Interwoven, heart to heart,
From this dance, we will not part.

With every rhythm, bonds grow tight,
In the shadows, we find light.
Together we forge a path so bright,
In this dance, all feels right.

Cherish the steps, the turns we take,
In the moment, the memories make.
Through the music, we come alive,
In this dance, our souls will thrive.

Symphony of the Unseen

In every heart, a melody waits,
Soft notes rising, it resonates.
To silence, we lend our ears,
In the shadows, our truth appears.

Strings of fate, they intertwine,
Crafting dreams, both yours and mine.
In the quiet, we can hear,
The symphony drawing near.

Harmonies blend, as lives connect,
Unseen pathways we reflect.
With every breath, the song unfolds,
In our hearts, its magic holds.

So let us dance to this sweet sound,
In the folds of love, we are found.
In the unseen, our spirits soar,
A symphony forevermore.

Every heartbeat plays its part,
Together creating, speak from the heart.
In this union, we are seen,
A beautiful, eternal dream.

Threads of Intersection

In the quiet web of fate,
Strands of life intertwine,
Moments mesh and resonate,
Creating paths divine.

Whispers shared in fleeting glances,
Destinies gently weave,
A dance of chance, subtle chances,
In every thread, believe.

Colors blend in harmony,
Patterns shift and sway,
Together crafting tapestry,
In shades of yesterday.

Each knot a story to unfold,
With love and laughter sewn,
As journeys shared, brave and bold,
In every heart, a home.

Embrace the ties that bind us close,
In this woven space we thrive,
For in our lives, we find our dose,
Of joy that keeps us alive.

The Echoes of Compassionate Hearts

In silence, kindness speaks loud,
A whisper of gentle care,
In crowded rooms or beneath a cloud,
Compassion's presence is rare.

Each smile a bridge, subtle and sweet,
Connecting souls, heart to heart,
In every gesture, love's heartbeat,
Compassion plays its part.

When shadows fall and tempests rise,
The warmth of grace still glows,
For in the depths, an echo lies,
Of kindness that flows.

Hands extended in times of need,
Bonds that break every pain,
With gentle strength, we plant the seed,
Of hope through every rain.

Together we'll rise, together we'll stand,
In unity's soft embrace,
With every heart lending a hand,
To build a better place.

Harbors of Kindred Spirits

In the stillness of the night,
We gather like the stars,
In conversations soft and bright,
Our dreams, like moons, are ours.

With every story shared, we grow,
A bond that knows no end,
In laughter's light or sorrow's flow,
Together we transcend.

These harbors built of trust and grace,
Embrace our weary souls,
A refuge found in every space,
Where love and kindness strolls.

In the ebb and flow of time,
We sail through storms and calm,
Each kindred spirit, a shared rhyme,
A soothing, gentle balm.

Together, we navigate the seas,
With hands held firm and tight,
In the warmth of friendship's breeze,
We find our true delight.

The Softness of Together's Embrace

In twilight glow, we find our peace,
In quiet moments, side by side,
With every heartbeat, our worries cease,
In togetherness, we abide.

A touch, a glance, like tender rain,
That nurtures every sprout,
In shared silence, we ease the pain,
Of world's relentless doubt.

The softness wraps around our hearts,
A blanket warm and wide,
In this cocoon, fear departs,
As love is our guide.

Together, through the thick and thin,
We stand with spirits high,
In the quiet strength that we begin,
Our souls forever tie.

With gentle whispers, dreams take flight,
In the haven of your arms,
We dance between the dark and light,
Safe from all the harms.

Guiding Stars in the Night

In the vast expanse above,
Twinkling lights of dreams and hope,
They whisper tales of love,
In dark, they help us cope.

Each star a path to follow,
A glimmer in the gloom,
With every soft and shallow,
The night begins to bloom.

A compass for the wayward,
Their shine, a gentle grace,
In shadows growing fabled,
They lead us to a place.

Through winter's chilly air,
And summer's dappled skies,
They remind us to beware,
Of fleeting time that flies.

So look up, take your heart,
Let the guiding stars unite,
In their glow, feel the spark,
And find your way through night.

The River that Connects

A ribbon of flowing blue,
Winding through the land so wide,
It carries whispers true,
Of all who gather by its side.

From mountains high and steep,
To valleys warm and kind,
It holds the secrets deep,
Of journeys intertwined.

With every gentle bend,
Stories woven in its flow,
Where strangers become friends,
And friendships start to grow.

The waters sing a tune,
A melody so sweet,
Reflecting the bright moon,
As hearts and rivers meet.

So follow where it leads,
Let it carry you each day,
For in its gentle reeds,
Connections come to play.

A Canvas of Shared Sunsets

Beneath the painted sky,
Colors blend with soft delight,
As day waves its goodbye,
In the warmth of fading light.

With hues of orange burn,
And splashes of deep red,
Every sunset teaches us,
That endings lie ahead.

A canvas shared with friends,
Where laughter fills the air,
In reflections, love transcends,
The moments that we share.

So gather close and dream,
As shadows start to creep,
In this brilliant beam,
Together, we'll keep.

Each sunset tells a tale,
Of life and love anew,
As stars begin to sail,
Our hearts find meaning true.

Voices in the Wind

The gentle breeze that calls,
Carries whispers from afar,
Through trees, it softly falls,
Like echoes of a star.

In every gust, a story,
Of lives and dreams once bold,
A tapestry of glory,
In each word, a treasure told.

Through meadows wild and free,
It dances with the leaves,
A symphony of glee,
As nature softly weaves.

So close your eyes and hear,
The secrets spirits send,
In the softest sphere,
Where thoughts and feelings blend.

For in each breath of air,
Lies wisdom from the past,
A harmony we share,
A moment built to last.

Canvas of Compassionate Steps

In shadows cast by tender hearts,
Each act of love, a work of art.
With every step, a gentle trace,
Compassion blooms in each warm space.

Together we paint, side by side,
In colors rich, our souls abide.
Through strokes of kindness, bright and clear,
A canvas filled with hope and cheer.

The whispers of the winds acknowledge,
In silence, we share every knowledge.
Hand in hand, we forge our fate,
Guided by love, never too late.

Like rivers flowing from the skies,
Our hopes ascend, they rise and rise.
The canvas stretched, it waits in awe,
Compassion's beauty, a sacred law.

In the end, what matters most,
The love we shared, the hearts we host.
A vivid scene of warmth and grace,
Together we thrive, our soul's embrace.

A Voyage of Gentle Currents

On waters soft, we set our sail,
With dreams like ships, we'll never fail.
Beneath the stars, the moonlight glows,
A journey where serenity flows.

The gentle waves, they hum a tune,
A lullaby beneath the moon.
Each ripple speaks of tales untold,
Of hearts united, brave and bold.

Through storms that come, we find our way,
With courage fierce, come what may.
The currents guide us to the land,
Where peace and joy, hand in hand.

We honor all the unseen shores,
With every wave, our spirit soars.
An odyssey of love profound,
In every heart, a safe haven found.

Together we traverse the deep,
With memories rich, our souls to keep.
A voyage born of gentle grace,
With love as our guide through time and space.

The Mosaic of Unspoken Bonds

In silence shared, our hearts collide,
A tapestry where dreams reside.
Each thread a story, woven tight,
In the glimmering of shared light.

Colors blend in gentle hue,
Every moment old and new.
With each glance, a secret told,
In the quiet, love unfolds.

This mosaic speaks without a word,
In the softest whispers heard.
Strength in unity, hand in hand,
A bond that time cannot disband.

Like fragments of a vast expanse,
We dance in life's intricate chance.
Together forming pieces rare,
In the stillness, love lays bare.

Through cracks of time, we intertwine,
In laughter bright, hearts align.
The mosaic shines, a vibrant glow,
A testament to love we know.

Underneath a Canopy of Trust

Beneath the boughs, we find our peace,
In nature's arms, our worries cease.
The leaves converse in breezy lines,
Trust glimmers softly, like rare signs.

Together here, we lay our fears,
Wrapped in laughter, joy appears.
Each whispered secret under trees,
Echoes softly, carried by breeze.

The roots run deep, in earth they bind,
A hidden strength, a love refined.
Through storms we stand, side by side,
In trust, our hearts are open wide.

Each branch above, a sheltering guide,
Where love and truth can coincide.
In moments shared, we rise and thrive,
Underneath this canopy, we live.

As seasons change, and time rolls on,
Our trust remains, forever strong.
In this embrace of nature's crust,
Together we flourish, filled with trust.

Traces of Whispered Connections

In the hush of twilight's grace,
Soft words linger in the air.
Echoes dance in hidden spaces,
A secret bond, forever rare.

Fingers brush in tender glances,
Time stills in a fleeting touch.
Heartbeats share the moonlit chances,
In silence, we discover much.

Though distance stretches like the sea,
Threads of gold connect our hearts.
Every thought, a melody,
In dreams, we play our parts.

Moments woven, strong yet slight,
Like shadows that the stars have cast.
We meet again in whispered light,
From the future, and the past.

A tapestry of fleeting sighs,
Designed in warmth and soft regret.
In the quiet truth that lies,
Our souls, forever intermet.

The Lightness of Shared Shadows

Walking under the ancient trees,
Our silhouettes begin to merge.
The laughter carried on the breeze,
A gentle, sweet and sacred surge.

Beneath the sun, our spirits glow,
Together, we embrace the sun.
With every step, our worries slow,
In this dance, we become one.

Casting aside our heavy doubts,
We find freedom in our play.
In stillness, doubt no longer shouts,
With shared shadows, we find our way.

Moments hinge on whispered light,
Navigating paths, side by side.
In unity, we take our flight,
Together, a lovely guide.

In the evening's calm embrace,
We gather warmth from stories told.
Lightness rests on every face,
In shared shadows, we are bold.

A Palette of Quiet Rememberings

Brushstrokes dance on canvas mild,
Colors soft, with shadows deep.
Every stroke, a memory compiled,
In stillness, time begins to seep.

Gentle hues of laughter's grace,
Blend with whispers of the past.
In each corner, a bright trace,
A legacy of joys amassed.

Strokes of sorrow paint the blue,
Yet muted tones bring solace round.
In every shade, a hope shines through,
A quiet beauty, softly found.

The palette sings of love and loss,
Mixed together for the heart.
In quiet moments, we pay the cost,
As each layer sets apart.

With every glance, a truth revealed,
In essence, we see our way.
A canvas rich and never healed,
In quiet rememberings, we stay.

The Art of Embracing Differences

In hues and shades we find our place,
Every color speaks its truth.
Together, we can interlace,
A picture vibrant, bold in youth.

Voices rise with varied tones,
In harmony, they find their song.
Celebrating all our zones,
In difference, we all belong.

What makes us unique is our grace,
A tapestry of life unfolds.
In acceptance, we embrace,
Our stories bright, yet never sold.

Through the prism of the heart,
Connections flourish, each a spark.
In unity, we play our part,
Lighting up the vibrant dark.

The art of love, a canvas wide,
Where every stroke brings forth the light.
With open arms, we choose to guide,
In embracing, we find our might.

The Harmonization of Silenced Voices

Whispers linger in the night,
Echoes lost, yet spirits bright.
Hearts unite, break the chains,
Songs of hope in soft refrains.

Through the shadows, truth shall crawl,
Silent cries, hear the call.
In the dark, we find our strength,
Harmonies rise, at length.

Voices merge, a vibrant spree,
Each a note in symphony.
Together loud, together proud,
Once alone, now beaming crowd.

In the stillness, promise lies,
From the ashes, voices rise.
Bound by dreams, we navigate,
In this space, we celebrate.

Bridges built across the fears,
Melodies wash away the tears.
Together forming brighter days,
In the song, our truth displays.

The Gathering of Kindred Souls

Underneath the glowing stars,
We find light and share our scars.
In this space, hearts beat as one,
Together here, our souls are spun.

Fingers touch and laughter rings,
In the joy each moment brings.
Kindred spirits drawn so near,
In the warmth, we share our cheer.

Stories told, both young and old,
In the circle, fears unfold.
Shared laughter and knowing glances,
Through the night, the magic dances.

Hands entwined, a sacred bond,
With each heartbeat, we grow fond.
In this union, we are whole,
Forever bound, each kindred soul.

As the dawn begins to sway,
We'll cherish this wondrous play.
In the gathering, love's embrace,
Together we'll find our place.

The Gentle Embrace of Shared Glances

In the quiet, eyes will meet,
A soft touch, a pulse discreet.
Silent stories, whispers flow,
In that glance, a world we know.

Flickers of warmth, holding tight,
In our gaze, we find the light.
Two souls woven, threads align,
In the silence, love's design.

Mornings bright, with hope anew,
Shared glances say, 'I see you.'
Unspoken words like gentle rain,
In the moment, joy and pain.

Through the rush and loud dismay,
In exchanged looks, we find our way.
Every glance, a comfort's tune,
Underneath the watchful moon.

In the dance of fleeting time,
Shared moments, a soothing rhyme.
In the depths of what we feel,
The gentle truth, our hearts reveal.

Pathways of Empathetic Exploration

Step by step, we wander wide,
In the footsteps of the tide.
Hearts open to what we find,
In the journey, love entwined.

Each experience, a shared plight,
Illuminating the night.
Hand in hand, through joy and pain,
In the storms, we'll still remain.

Listening close, we hear their cries,
Seeing worlds through others' eyes.
With compassion, we unfold,
Stories rich and tales retold.

On this path, we grow and learn,
For the fire of hope shall burn.
Empathy, our guiding star,
In the wild, we travel far.

Together we will build a road,
In each heart, we lay the code.
For in unity, we thrive,
In exploration, we come alive.

In the Realm of Gentle Echoes

In twilight's hush, whispers sigh,
Softly weaving through the sky.
Dreams dance lightly on the breeze,
A melody of heart's unease.

Beneath the stars, shadows creep,
In memories that gently weep.
A touch, a glance, in softest glow,
Where secrets of the night do flow.

Through fragile threads of time we tread,
In cozy nooks where kindness spread.
Each echo lingers, sweet and clear,
In the silence, love draws near.

In this realm of gentle grace,
We find ourselves, we find our place.
A tapestry of thoughts entwined,
In heartfelt bonds, we are combined.

Thus, we linger, shadows played,
In soft reflections, memories made.
With gentle echoes, we will roam,
In unison, we find our home.

A Pathway to Radiant Connections

Beneath the arch of lofty trees,
A pathway forms with every breeze.
With every step, the world we greet,
Where strangers and friends shall meet.

Sunlight dances on the ground,
In gentle laughter, joy is found.
With open hearts, we take the lead,
To nurture every loving seed.

Each story shared, a thread of gold,
In warmth and trust, our hearts unfold.
Through paths diverged, yet we align,
In unity, our spirits shine.

In moments fleeting, bonds create,
Together we can navigate.
For every soul holds light inside,
In radiant connections, we abide.

Let kindness flow with every stride,
A pathway built where dreams reside.
In every heart, a space awaits,
To share our lives, to celebrate.

Quiet Ripples of Shared Existence

In tranquil waters, reflections play,
Softest whispers guide the way.
Each ripple speaks of dreams and fears,
As time weaves gently with our years.

Through whispered sighs, we come alive,
In our stories, we will thrive.
Connections bloom, tender and bright,
In the silence, we find our light.

Each moment shared, a treasured gift,
In quiet spaces, our spirits lift.
With every touch, a bond we tie,
In this existence, you and I.

Through valleys deep and mountains high,
In shared existence, we dare to fly.
With open hearts, we break the mold,
In quiet ripples, our truths unfold.

As twilight settles, we find our peace,
In whispered dreams, our worries cease.
With every heartbeat, we will know,
Together, as the ripples flow.

The Weaving of Parallel Stories

In threads of life, our tales entwine,
Two paths converge, a dance divine.
With every heartbeat, stories blend,
In the weaving, we transcend.

In laughter shared, and tears that fall,
Each moment captured, we recall.
Through epochs vast, our spirits soar,
In parallel journeys, we explore.

With colors bright, our lives displayed,
In every twist, a choice is made.
Through winding roads and open skies,
In the tapestry of love, we rise.

Together we craft our destinies,
In the fabric of life's memories.
Every thread glimmers, bold and true,
In the weaving, me and you.

So let us cherish every line,
In this great story, I am thine.
For in our hearts, the truth will show,
The weaving of love will ever grow.

Whispers of Balance

In the quiet night, stars align,
Shadows dance softly, so divine.
Hearts find rhythm in gentle sway,
Nature whispers, guiding the way.

A breeze carries secrets untold,
Embracing the warmth as we grow old.
In harmony, we find our place,
A tapestry woven with grace.

The moonlight glimmers on the stream,
Reflecting hopes and every dream.
In stillness, we learn to embrace,
The beauty of life, the cosmic chase.

With every heartbeat, we connect,
Threads of patience and respect.
In whispers of balance, we shall see,
The strength in unity, you and me.

Together we rise, united we stand,
Carving futures, hand in hand.
In every moment, let's celebrate,
The whispers of balance that fate create.

Echoes of Unity

A chorus of voices fills the air,
Each note a promise, a bond we share.
Together we sing, hearts intertwined,
In echoes of unity, peace we find.

Through laughter and tears, we pave the way,
In every challenge, together we stay.
With open arms and tender hearts,
We find our strength as the journey starts.

From mountains high to valleys low,
In every step, our spirits glow.
With every echo, we lift one another,
For every sister, every brother.

The rhythm of life beats strong and true,
In every hue, a vibrant view.
In echoes profound, we connect and thrive,
With unity's warmth, we come alive.

Let our voices rise, like birds at dawn,
In this song of togetherness, we are reborn.
With every note, let love be our guide,
In the echoes of unity, we take pride.

The Pathway of Togetherness

A winding road beneath our feet,
Footsteps echo, a comforting beat.
Through storms and sun, we journey on,
In the pathway of togetherness, never alone.

With every challenge that we face,
In unity, we find our grace.
Hand in hand, we weave our fate,
Through every twist, we celebrate.

The road may be long, but hope lights the way,
In each other's strength, we'll boldly stay.
Through every valley, we'll rise and soar,
Together we'll open every door.

In laughter and love, we lift our voice,
In togetherness, we make our choice.
A journey shared, through thick and thin,
In this great dance, we must begin.

So take my hand, let's forge ahead,
On the pathway of togetherness we tread.
In every step, a promise we find,
For together, our hearts are designed.

Melodies of Serendipity

In unexpected moments, joy appears,
Life hums a tune, dissolving fears.
With every laugh, a new refrain,
In melodies of serendipity, we gain.

Through twists of fate, paths intertwine,
Caught in the magic of the divine.
Shared smiles echo in the air,
Moments cherished beyond compare.

As starlit skies embrace the night,
Our hearts dance freely, pure delight.
In the melodies, we find our way,
Guided by love, come what may.

With every heartbeat, serendipity sings,
Life's sweetest treasures that simply spring.
In laughter and light, let's forge ahead,
To the rhythm of dreams that we've said.

In the symphony of life, never shy,
We find our wings and learn to fly.
In every note, a chance to be,
In the melodies of serendipity.

The Brushstrokes of Reunion

Fingers brush against the past,
Memories painted, fading fast.
Colors blend in joyful cheer,
Hearts unite, the end is near.

Whispers linger in the air,
Echoes of love, ever rare.
Frames adorned with laughter's thread,
Canvas bright, where hope is spread.

Time suspends, the world holds breath,
Rekindled flames defy all death.
With each stroke, a bond restored,
A treasure trove, hearts explored.

Silent glances tell the tale,
Through storms and winds, we shall not fail.
In this gallery of our days,
Love's portrait shines in countless ways.

Together, drawing lines anew,
With every hue, affection grew.
Hand in hand, we paint our dreams,
In vibrant shades, love's gentle gleams.

A Tidal Wave of Shared Affection

Waves crash softly on the shore,
Hearts collide, forevermore.
Ocean's depth in every glance,
A dance of souls, a sweet romance.

Rippling tides of laughter rise,
Reflections sparkle in our eyes.
Shores embrace, the story's told,
With every wave, love's warmth unfolds.

Salty air and whispers sweet,
In each heartbeat, our souls meet.
The ebb and flow of time sustained,
A boundless sea, where love remains.

Cascading moments, pure delight,
In tidal pools, our dreams ignite.
Together we will brave the sea,
A wave of love, wild and free.

Tides may shift and sands may part,
Yet you will always fill my heart.
An ocean's promise, deep and wide,
In shared affection, we abide.

The Celestial Dance of Life's Interplay

Stars align in velvet night,
Galaxies twirl, a wondrous sight.
Planets play their ancient song,
In this dance, we all belong.

Nebulae bloom with colors bright,
Life unfolds in cosmic light.
Every heartbeat, every sigh,
A rhythm in the endless sky.

Fleeting moments, intertwined,
In this waltz, our fates unbind.
Gravity pulls, yet we transcend,
Together, we will never end.

Comets streak, igniting dreams,
In the dark, our brilliance gleams.
Constellations tell our tale,
A cosmic bond that will not pale.

With every turn, we spin and sway,
In life's grand ballet, come what may.
Celestial bodies, love so rare,
In this interplay, we're laid bare.

Solar Flares of Embraced Differences

Sunlight breaks through clouds above,
Illuminating paths of love.
Diversity in radiant hues,
Each unique, yet we all choose.

Solar flares ignite the sky,
A burst of colors, you and I.
In every shade, we find our place,
With open hearts, we embrace grace.

Waves of warmth in laughter shared,
Different stories, we have bared.
Yet in the light, we stand as one,
In differences, we've just begun.

Roots entwined in fertile ground,
Love can flourish all around.
Golden rays, they illuminate,
A tapestry we cultivate.

With every flare, our spirits soar,
In unity, we seek for more.
Together, shining ever bright,
Embraced by love, in shared light.

Chasing the Golden Sun

In dawn's embrace, we rise anew,
With colors bright, the world in view.
Golden rays dance on the sea,
Whispers of dreams, wild and free.

Footprints trace the sanded shore,
Chasing light forevermore.
Each wave sings a gentle tune,
Promises made beneath the moon.

The sky ignites, a fiery ball,
Time stands still, we heed its call.
In twilight's glow, we gather near,
Hearts aflame, casting out fear.

With laughter shared, our spirits soar,
Chasing the sun, we ask for more.
In every sunset, hope remains,
A cycle bound, yet never chains.

Together every dawn we greet,
The golden sun, a heartbeat sweet.
In harmony, we find our way,
Chasing the light of a brand new day.

Tides of Solace

Waves caress the quiet shore,
Soft as a whisper, they implore.
In the stillness, hearts entwine,
Finding peace in the ocean's sign.

Wandering thoughts like driftwood flow,
Carried by currents, gentle and slow.
The rhythm of tides, a balm for pain,
In waters deep, we break the chain.

Shells and stones, treasures to find,
Reflecting memories left behind.
With every ebb, with every flow,
Time reveals what we need to know.

Together we stand, hand in hand,
In the solace of this endless sand.
With the tide, let worries fade,
In the embrace of the ocean's shade.

Each sunset brings a new refrain,
Of tides that soothe, of love's domain.
In the depths, our souls align,
Finding solace in your heart's design.

The Confluence of Souls

Where rivers meet and waters blend,
The stories told shall never end.
In this place, our spirits rise,
Reflecting light from myriad skies.

With every glance, a bond is forged,
In the current, love is surged.
Currents pulsing, hearts in sync,
Together as one, we breathe and think.

As shadows cast beneath the trees,
We find our peace in whispered leaves.
The symphony of life unfolds,
In gentle waves, our truth it holds.

At twilight's hour, we pause and dream,
In the confluence, we become a theme.
Each heartbeat echoes pure and true,
A testament to me and you.

As the night descends, we stay aligned,
In the stillness, hearts unconfined.
Where rivers meet, our souls embrace,
In this sacred, timeless space.

Beneath the Canopy of Together

In the embrace of emerald leaves,
Whispers of nature, the heart believes.
Roots entwined, we stand so tall,
Beneath the canopy, we feel it all.

Sunlight dapples, a gentle kiss,
Moments treasured, purest bliss.
Together we walk, hand in hand,
In this sacred, enchanted land.

Birds in flight, a melody sweet,
Nature's symphony beneath our feet.
With every sigh, the world grows still,
Under the trees, we drink our fill.

Seasons change, and yet we stay,
In the warmth of love, come what may.
In shadows cast, our dreams take flight,
Beneath the canopy, hearts ignited bright.

Forever bound in heart and soul,
Together we strive for a common goal.
In the depths of forests, side by side,
Beneath the canopy, our dreams abide.

The Serenade of Togetherness

In the glow of gentle light,
Two hearts dance in pure delight,
With whispers soft as evening breeze,
Bound by love, they find their ease.

Through the valleys and the hills,
Hand in hand, their spirit thrills,
Each note sung in harmony,
A song of sweet unity.

Moments shared, both joy and pain,
They weather storms, embrace the rain,
In laughter's warmth, in silence deep,
Together, promises they keep.

As twilight wraps the day in gold,
Such stories of love unfold,
In every gaze, a timeless tune,
A serenade beneath the moon.

Through years that pass, like shifting sands,
Together still, they make their plans,
In every heart, a song to sing,
The serenade of everything.

Chasing Echoes in the Twilight

Beneath the sky where shadows play,
We chase the echoes of the day,
With every step, the whispers call,
In twilight's glow, we feel it all.

The fading light, a fleeting spark,
We wander pathways, brave the dark,
Each echo holds a tale to tell,
In silence shared, we fell and fell.

With hearts aligned, we seek the truth,
In the twilight, we find our youth,
Chasing dreams like fireflies bright,
Illuminating the quiet night.

The world asleep, yet spirits rise,
In whispered thoughts and starlit skies,
Together, we dance on the edge,
Chasing echoes, we make our pledge.

With every breath, we find our way,
In twilight's arms, come what may,
Chasing echoes, hand in hand,
In this moment, we take a stand.

Reflections in Still Waters

In the calm of morning light,
The waters gleam, so pure, so bright,
Each ripple tells a tale of days,
Reflections dance in subtle ways.

The world above, a canvas spun,
Mirrored beauty, endless run,
In stillness, secrets intertwine,
With nature's brush, the heart designs.

Through whispers soft, the breezes flow,
In mirrored depths, emotions glow,
Every glance, a fleeting sigh,
In still waters, moments lie.

As twilight fades, the stars appear,
In quiet night, the world is clear,
With every shimmer, time stands still,
Reflections soft, our hearts fulfill.

In love and dreams, we dive so deep,
In still waters, promises keep,
With every wave, our spirits soar,
Reflecting life, forevermore.

The Unison of Life's Canvas

Upon the canvas, colors blend,
With every stroke, the stories send,
Life's journey etched in hues so bright,
A masterpiece in shared delight.

Each moment, like a vibrant hue,
Together, we craft something new,
In laughter's glow and sorrow's shade,
A unison of dreams displayed.

Through trials faced and joy embraced,
We find the beauty, we interlace,
Our brushstrokes weaving tales so grand,
The canvas stretches, hand in hand.

In every tear, a rainbow shines,
In every heart, life's love entwines,
An artful dance of give and take,
The unison, a bond we make.

As seasons change, new colors pour,
Together, we explore the core,
With every heartbeat, brush and pen,
Life's canvas blooms, again and again.

The Symphony of Kindred Spirits

In the quiet of the night,
Harmony drifts in flight.
Voices whisper sweet and low,
Hearts entwined in gentle flow.

Under stars that brightly gleam,
We are stitched in every dream.
Shared laughter fills the air,
Moments that we long to share.

Each note played, a tale unfolds,
Connections made, as warmth enfolds.
In the dance of light and shade,
Our symphony will never fade.

Through the storms and calm, we find,
Gentle hands that are aligned.
Together in this boundless sea,
Forever woven, you and we.

As the seasons shift and sway,
Kindred spirits, here we stay.
In this melody of life,
We cherish love beyond the strife.

Cascading Notes of Delight

A gentle breeze begins to play,
Chasing clouds and thoughts away.
Dancing leaves in vibrant hues,
Nature's call sings bright and true.

The brook hums a soft refrain,
Echoing through sweet terrain.
Each drop falling, pure and clear,
Brings the heart a sense of cheer.

With every flutter, bees take flight,
Their buzzing adds to the delight.
Sunshine warms the waking ground,
In this bliss, joy can be found.

Through the gardens, laughter flows,
In harmony, affection grows.
Cascading notes of joyful song,
Remind us where we all belong.

Embrace the moments, feel the zest,
With open hearts, we are blessed.
In each corner, love ignites,
Cascading notes, our spirits' flights.

A Tapestry of Connected Lives

Threads of passion, colors blend,
Woven stories that we send.
In the fabric, lessons sewn,
In the hearts, seeds of hope grown.

Through gold and gray, joy and pain,
Each experience, a thread's gain.
On this loom, we craft our fate,
Designs of love and hopes create.

In laughter's weave and silence deep,
Vows and promises we keep.
Connected lives through every stitch,
In the tapestry, we find our niche.

Moments shared in twilight's glow,
A piece of you, a piece of me, too.
Together, we shape our space,
In this pattern, we embrace.

So let us cherish what we find,
As threads of destiny entwined.
In the heart, our stories thrive,
A masterpiece of connected lives.

Finding Balance Amongst Chaos

In the whirlwind, we lose sight,
Calm emerges from the night.
Finding stillness in the fray,
Guiding hearts along the way.

When the world spins fast and wild,
Pause to breathe, like a child.
In chaos, seek the gentle tune,
A quiet calm, an afternoon.

Amidst the noise, we find our voice,
In every choice, we make rejoice.
Balance sought through trials past,
Strength in unity, we hold fast.

With open minds and beating hearts,
We weave the chaos into arts.
In the journey, lessons learned,
In shadows deep, our light returned.

So let us dance on shifting ground,
In harmony, we'll stand our ground.
Through the chaos, paths we pave,
Finding balance, we will be brave.